# Canadian Psycho

The True Story of Luka Magnotta

*Volume V*

by Cara Lee Carter

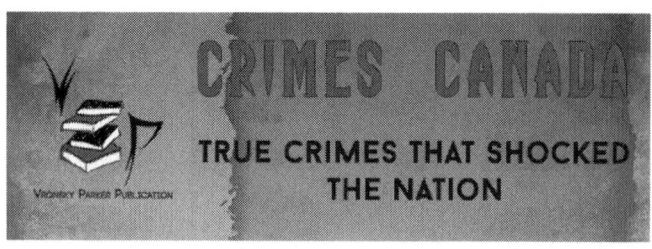

# Canadian Psycho

The True Story of Luka Magnotta

*Volume V*

**by Cara Lee Carter**

**Crimes Canada
True Crimes That Shocked The Nation**

**ISBN**-13: 978-1515117506
**ISBN**-10: 1515117502

Copyright and Published (2015)

VP Publications an imprint of
RJ Parker Publishing, Inc.

*Published in Canada*

# Copyrights

This book is licensed for your personal enjoyment only. This book may not be re-sold or given away to other people. If you would like to share this book with another person, please purchase an additional copy for each recipient. If you are reading this book and did not purchase it, or it was not purchased for your use only, then please return to the author and purchase your own copy. Thank you for respecting the hard work of the author. All rights reserved. No part of this publication can be reproduced or transmitted in any form or by any means without prior written authorization from Peter Vronsky or RJ Parker of VP Publications and RJ Parker Publishing, Inc. The unauthorized reproduction or distribution of a copyrighted work is illegal. Criminal copyright infringement, including infringement without monetary gain, is investigated by the FBI and is punishable by fines and federal imprisonment.

# Crimes Canada: True Crimes That Shocked the Nation *Series Introduction*

This is multi-volume twenty-four book collection, (one per month, each approximately 100 to 170 pages) project, by crime historian Dr. Peter Vronsky and true crime author and publisher RJ Parker, depicting some of Canada's most notorious criminals.

Crimes Canada: True Crimes that Shocked the Nation will feature a series of Canadian true crime short-read books published by VP Publications (Vronsky & Parker), an imprint of *RJ Parker Publishing, Inc.*, one of North America's leading publishers of true crime.

Peter Vronsky is the bestselling author of *Serial Killers: The Method and Madness of Monsters* and *Female Serial Killers: How and Why Women Become Monsters* while RJ Parker is not only a successful publisher but also the author of 18 books, including *Serial Killers Abridged: An Encyclopedia of 100 Serial Killers*, *Parents Who Killed Their Children: Filicide*, and *Serial Killer Groupies*. Both are Canadians and have teamed up to share shocking Canadian true crime cases not only with fellow Canadian readers but with Americans and world readers as well, who will be shocked and horrified by just how evil and sick "nice" Canadians can be when they go bad.

Finally, we invite fellow Canadians, aspiring or established authors, to submit proposals or manuscripts to VP Publications at *Editors@CrimesCanada.com*.

VP Publications is a new frontier traditional publisher, offering their published authors a generous royalty agreement payable within three months of publishing and aggressive online marketing support. Unlike many so-called "publishers" that are nothing but vanity presses in disguise, VP Publications does not charge authors in advance for submitting their proposal or manuscripts, nor do we charge authors if we choose to publish their works. We pay you, and pay well.

Enjoy these top rated true crime eBooks from VP Publications **FREE** as part of your Kindle Unlimited subscription. You can read it on your Kindle Fire, on a computer via Kindle Cloud Reader or on any smartphone with the free Kindle reading app.

**View All True Crime and Crime Fiction Books by RJ Parker Publishing at the following Amazon Links:**

*Amazon Kindle - USA*
*Amazon Kindle - Canada*
*Amazon Kindle - UK*
*Amazon Kindle - Australia*

**NOTE:** quoted words in *italics* are verbatim and therefore any typos or grammatical errors are left intact.

# Birth or Making of a Psychopath?
*Introduction by RJ Parker*

Luka Magnotta was not a serial killer, as he didn't kill two or more people that we know of. But he would have if not captured.

He was dubbed the 'Canadian Psycho' for a reason, and I'm certain once you've read this book, you'll agree that he was a psychopath, a diagnosis that some doctors in Canada dismissed in his case.

I might add that not all psychopaths are killers, or even criminals. Everyone probably dated one in their life, or worked for or with one. Some psychopaths can harness their disorder toward a successful career where sometimes having no regard for the feelings of others can be advantageous: corporate CEOs, politicians, entertainers and even yes, true crime authors, can be full-blown psychopaths. Most of us have encountered one or two somewhere in our lives.

***

Psychopaths represent around one percent of the world's population, which means that one out of every hundred people is a psychopath. In contrast to this, about twenty-five percent of the world's prison population is comprised of those who have shown psychopathic tendencies, one out of every four people. This disproportionate ratio shows just how serious psychopathy is.

Because of the pervasive nature of psychological state in modern popular culture, with every other antagonist in television programming, books and movies displaying psychopathic tendencies, there has been much interest in the scientific community as well as the general public in the origin of this mental illness.

Another reason for this interest in psychopaths is the horrific manner in which they commit their crimes. The crimes being spoken of here are cold blooded and serial murders which are what psychopaths are best known for and most often associated with. A serial killer murders in cold blood, does so obsessively and compulsively for no reason other than pleasure. They are brutal, creatively so, and are often without remorse. Hence, the serial killer is often the subject of morbid curiosity. They are seen as horrific examples of what happens when the gates of amorality are flung open; they show people what could happen if they lose all sense of empathy.

Hence, people want to know what brings about this state of being, this way of thinking that demeans one's fellow man to the point where one would brutalize and murder them, often after sexually violating them. What leads to this form of depravity, and can it be stopped?

In order to ascertain what it is that makes psychopaths behave the way that they do, it is important to first understand what exactly a psychopath is. An understanding of a psychopath's state of mind is essential because it helps us understand the theories behind what makes a psychopath tick.

There are several personality traits that psychopaths possess. Any individual that has a combination of these personality traits probably suffers from some form of psychopathy. These personality traits include:

1) A lack of empathy. Essentially an absence of remorse or guilt after having caused someone pain or harm.

2) Lack of an ability to feel profound emotions. Psychopaths tend not to feel love, only passing affection at most.

3) Lack of inhibitions or impulse control. Psychopaths tend to have little ability to defer gratification.

4) An inflated sense of self worth or an overly large ego. Psychopaths tend to think very highly of themselves.

5) A refusal to accept responsibility for their actions, and a perpetual internal narrative that others are responsible for the pain they cause.

Psychopaths aren't all violent, but they do seem to be socially destructive and tend to lean towards substance abuse.

There are two major theories behind what leads to psychopathy. These two theories pertain to two aspects of what shapes the human personality: nature and nurture. Though there are various other complex factors at work, the origin of the psychopath boils down to one of these two factors, or a combination of both in some cases.

## **Nature:**

What is nature exactly? It can be defined as the work of God if you are religiously inclined. It can be described as the end result of millennia of evolution. All in all, proponents of the nature theory tend to believe that the psychopath is the way he is due to the fact that he was born that way.

What this means is that psychopathy is a disorder of the brain. This disorder is at various times considered to be chemical or physical. A chemical disorder that leads to psychopathy generally means that the psychopath suffers from an excess of testosterone, leading to increased and unnatural aggression, or a general imbalance in the chemical structure of his brain. This excess in testosterone is often also accompanied by low levels of serotonin in the brain, a chemical that tends to cause euphoria and a sense of peace. As a result of this combination, psychopaths are very aggressive, and do not feel satisfied easily. Releasing their aggression gives them a boost in the serotonin levels of their brain, and since the levels of serotonin are naturally low, these psychopaths end up performing great acts of violence in order to feel its effects.

Alternatively, many proponents of the nature argument claim that psychopaths think the way they do because their brains are different structurally as well as chemically. Psychopaths have either enlarged or malformed amygdalas. The amygdala is the section of the brain that processes our emotional reactions and helps us with decision making. A malformed and thus malfunctioning amygdala can thus clearly cause a lot of the problems psychopaths face, such as impaired judgement due to inherently poor decision making as well as a severe impairment of the way they process emotions. One of the major ways that this affects their personalities is through exacerbating the aforementioned testosterone overload. Too much testosterone leads to wanton aggression. An inability to properly process this anger leads to a compounding of said aggression, thereby resulting in the creation of a vicious cycle that eventually leads to the violence that psychopaths are so famous for.

Psychopaths are also said to be created in the womb as a result of genetic anomalies. Studies conducted on psychopaths have suggested the presence of a recurrent genetic trait common in most if not all individuals displaying psychopathic tendencies. This suggests that psychopathy is hereditary, something that several studies have proven to be true. A particular gene is often considered to be responsible for psychopathic behavior. This gene, monoamine oxidase A, often called the warrior gene, exists in people that possess a desire for dominance over others as well as aggressive tendencies in pursuit of the aforementioned domination. The traits of those possessing this warrior gene are often surprisingly similar to those possessing psychopathic tendencies. This theory that psychopathy is the result of genetic anomalies ties in with the nurture theory as well, as these genetic anomalies can be compounded and exacerbated by environmental factors.

## Nurture:

Those that claim that one's nurturing is what eventually turns one into a psychopath postulate that psychopaths are made, not born. This theory is based on the fact that so many individuals exhibiting psychopathic behavior come from abusive homes, or from situations where they were desensitized to violence at an early age.

Studies conducted on individuals exhibiting psychopathic traits seem to confirm this to some extent. One study conducted on teenagers living in London showing signs of psychopathic behavior, confirmed a correlation between psychopathy and growing up with the following environmental conditions:

1) One or both parents convicted of a crime

2) Physical neglect during childhood

3) Absence of a father figure during upbringing

4) Maternal figure exhibiting signs of depression

5) Poverty or poor living conditions while growing up

6) Harsh discipline bordering on abuse

7) Lack of supervision while growing up

This study contended that it was these elements of the psychopath's upbringing that instilled in an individual the aggression that would cause him to commit such atrocious acts of violence. Another study suggested a link between psychopathy and an inability to integrate into society. Although it is unknown if the behavior causes the disorder, or if the disorder causes the behavior, but a correlation has been made between poor social skills and the development of psychopathic tendencies in later life. This is due to the mental impact negative treatment from one's peers can cause, negative treatment which can be reasoned by a failure to integrate.

Apart from upbringing, psychopathy has also been connected to injuries caused during childhood. Trauma caused to the head can end up resulting in brain damage. As has been mentioned in the nature argument, a damaged or malformed amygdala can result in an inability to process strong emotions. Damage done to the amygdala at such a young age can cause psychopathic tendencies later on in life.

The theory that psychopathy is caused by nurture also fits in with some nature arguments, in particular the theory that psychopathic behavior is caused by genetic anomalies. Certain studies have concluded that if an individual possesses psychopathic genes, then the way they are brought up can end up activating the behavior stored in these genes and unleashing the psychopath. It is also speculated that, if psychopathy were genetic, growing up with a psychopath for a parent can cause the development of psychopathic tendencies even if the individual is not genetically inclined to that sort of behavior.

All in all, it is probably a combination of both nature and nurture that cause psychopathic behavior. The depraved acts of serial and cold-blooded killers must require them to have a different kind of brain to allow them to dispense with empathy so easily and commit such horrendous acts of violence. However, the fact that so many killers grow up suffering abuse themselves implies that upbringing plays a strong role in molding the innocent child into the monster that he will one day become.

# Background

**In May 2012**, a janitor found a maggot-laced suitcase in a pile of rubbish outside of a low-rent apartment building in the Montreal neighborhood of Côte-des-Neiges. After opening the case, the grisly discovery was made of a dismembered human torso, peppered with stab wounds. The evidence collected by police would lead them too late to the door of a pornographic actor and escort who had fled the country after the slaying. During the course of their investigation, police discovered the murderer not only filmed his crime, but also posted the video depicting his heinous acts online for the world to see.

Murder, necrophilia, cannibalism and an international manhunt – while the tale of Luka Magnotta reads more like a work of fiction, the horrific murder and dismemberment of 32-year-old international Concordia student Lin Jun was, in fact, a documentary scripted by an individual with a long history of mental illness in a gruesome attempt to gain notoriety. Luka's history is littered with instances where he did everything possible to gain fame: trying out for reality television shows, lying about being connected to a well-known Canadian serial murderess, committing and filming acts of animal cruelty and, posting these videos on the Internet. His actions obviously exhibiting a continuous downward spiral.

Despite gaining the attention and ire of animal activists, it still wasn't enough to satisfy Luka's immense thirst for attention. He even went so far as to brag to a journalist about his intention to murder a person months before he actually committed the crime.

Magnotta took those final steps to gain name recognition, not only by committing the murder, but also the unthinkable act of posting the video and its indignities he committed on the victim. This video, uploaded to Canadian company Bestgore, quickly went viral via social media, attracting over 300,000 views in just four hours. As news broke about the dismemberment and subsequent video, it shocked and captivated not only the nation but also the entire world.

From the time the body was discovered, to the following international manhunt, the capture of Magnotta, and through the ensuing two years it took for justice to be served, the country anxiously waited for the outcome of the controversial trial. True to his many-sided persona, this book chronicles the journey that led Luka Magnotta to become known as the Cannibal Porn Star, the Butcher of Montreal and the Canadian Psycho.

# The Early Years

**Luka Rocco Magnotta** was born Eric Clinton Kirk Newman on July 24, 1982 in Scarborough, Ontario. His parents, Anna Yourkin and Donald Newman met while they were teenagers; she became pregnant shortly thereafter and moved into Donald's parents' basement after they were married. They named their first-born child after actors Clint Eastwood and Kirk Douglas, perhaps displaying an eerie intuition about their son's future obsession with fame. Just ten months after the arrival of their first-born, they welcomed another son, Conrad, followed by daughter Melissa a few years after that. Despite not having graduated from high school herself, dropping out when she became pregnant in Grade 9, Anna insisted on homeschooling their children.

For several years, they had no contact with kids their own age, and Donald claims his wife was controlling of their children. Eric would later describe his mother as "a woman obsessed with cleanliness, often wearing a surgical mask, rubber gloves and repeatedly washing her children's hands."[1] He alleges that his mother abused and isolated him, and at times would lock him and his siblings out of the house or car. He told a psychologist in one instance that she caused their pet rabbit's death by putting it outside during the winter, and that she would dress him in female clothing when he was younger. He also asserted that she made him wear diapers when he was 6-years-old because he still had difficulty not wetting the bed at night. He recalled being scared of his mother and says she tied his brother to a chair in his room when he was bad.

However, Eric did have a close relationship with his grandmother, Phyllis, on his mother's side, whom he felt raised him, but he would later say his grandmother would sleep in the same bed with him during those formative early years. This may have caused Eric some mental confusion, as he recalls that even at a young age, he wanted to be a girl. He would dress in his mother's clothing and use makeup when he was about 10-years-old which sexually aroused him. Even in his teenage years, he would try on his grandmother's bras and use mascara on his eyes. He played with Barbie dolls and said his grandmother called him a faggot and gave him dirty looks when he wore makeup. Eric would later say his family did not like how he dressed and made fun of his effeminate tone of voice, his hair and the way he crossed his legs.

As mentioned in the introduction, the advocates of the nurture theory for psychopathy argue that many killers are defined by their childhood. Consider the possibility that his homeschooling resulted in a lack of social skills, the fact that his mother was controlling, that killers seek control over their victims, and his problem with bedwetting, and subsequent bullying because of it, it's not surprising Eric went on to kill. According to serial killer expert, RJ Parker, if Eric had not been captured in Europe, it's quite likely he would have become a serial killer.

Donald and Anna lost the family's home when they couldn't keep up the mortgage payments, so they occasionally lived with their in-laws. Donald developed a serious drinking problem, and was fired from his factory job for drinking alcohol at work. These factors caused their marriage to end when Eric was 13-years-old. After the divorce, Anna and the children moved in with her mother Phyllis and the move brought about the Newman children's first formal education. They finally started attending school in 1992, with Eric starting in Grade 6 at Charlottetown Junior School. His educational records indicate he had difficulties with spoken and written language, math skills, confidence and social interaction upon entering the educational system. Described as both awkward and shy, Eric also suffered from acne. These factors, combined with diminutive interaction with children his own age and a deep-seated need to fabricate stories of magnificence about his life, caused a young Eric to be bullied and beat up. Later he explained that the other children made fun of his clothes, called him names such as gay and faggot, and would mess up his hair. For Eric, his time in school was torturous, and he said he was ostracised by his peers. However, a Grade 7 classmate of Eric's described him as a sad little kid who was small, immature and odd for his age, but "*almost too odd to be a target*" for bullying. She recalled he spent time with other socially awkward kids but didn't speak much and was shy. Eric was evaluated as under-functioning by at least two academic years, and he was placed in special education classes in Grade 9. He seemed to hold himself apart from other kids, had a negative view of himself, and was highly sensitive to criticism.

While Eric met anguish during his time in school, his father faced his own demons – Donald was hearing voices, delusional, feeling angry, and was suicidal. Doctors believed he was bipolar and he was initially diagnosed as manic-depressive. Years later he would be diagnosed as a paranoid schizophrenic manic-depressive and receive treatment with numerous anti-psychotic prescription drugs.

# Drunk on Ego

**From 1998-2000**, Eric attended I.E. Weldon Secondary School in Lindsay, a town in southeastern Ontario. Looking back, classmates and teachers recalled his vanity and obsession with his looks. Years later, in an interview for a reality television show, Eric admitted that even as a teenager people would tell him he was vain and always had to look in any mirror he passed by, lending credence to one of his diagnoses after he committed his infamous crime. At age 16, Eric suffered some verbal and physical abuse ("manhandling and physical intimidation") at the hands of his stepfather. He moved in with his grandmother for a while and then lived with his father.

Life got even more difficult for Eric at the age of 18. Following in his father's footsteps, he too started hearing voices and was brought to the hospital by his grandmother. During the April 2001 visit to the emergency department of Ross Memorial Hospital, Eric's behavior was described by a doctor as "bizarre", and just a few weeks later, he was diagnosed as a paranoid schizophrenic.

After dropping out of high school, he was employed in a number of dead-end jobs, but they never lasted long. He went on welfare, then started receiving disability support payments and was admitted to Harrison House, a psychiatric group home. He often complained of hallucinations, confusion and paranoid thinking, and even thought the government was following him and bugging his phone. [2]

Four months later, in August 2001, Eric was back at this hospital but this time for an overdose. A staff member of Harrison House noticed his odd behavior one day and realized he had overdosed on his recently filled prescription of Clonazepam.[3] Appointments with those in the medical profession became the norm for Eric – including a March 2003 visit where he and his father were both being treated at the same hospital for hearing voices. The next ten years would account for dozens of hospital visits to numerous doctors in both Canada and the United States. His home life fared no better with Eric occasionally living with his mother, or father, or his grandmother. There was little stability as he bounced around, living in places such as Toronto, New York and Los Angeles.

While in his early 20s, Eric began his career in the sex trade by creating pornography videos through the Internet with webcams but says he gave it up because there were too many crazy people. In 2002 he became a stripper at Remington's in Toronto (although the establishment has said they have no documentation of this association). Keeping with his trend of being unable to hold a steady job for long, he only lasted two months as a stripper. He followed that up by working as an escort and said he was sometimes raped during that career. Eric branched out into the world of pornographic films, acting in two films as a straight man "turned" gay. But even then, Eric harbored dark thoughts. He met and briefly dated transgender performance artist, Nina Arsenault, who recalls that during their time together, he made really bad jokes about drowning kittens and wanting to hurt people. *"He said he would do anything to be famous. I didn't think he meant killing someone. I thought he meant being a porn star, you know, exploiting his sex life. I think he did that for a long time and then he needed to do something new."*[4] She said after watching his infamous kill video, she felt he was performing the role of a psychopath because he wanted to be legendary. *"While Luka's actions are very extreme, I don't think it's an extreme desire for people in our culture to want to be famous. Something that is particularly macabre to me about Luka's situation is he did these thing to show them, and it seems like the situation is really a kind of serial killing or kind of sociopathic that is emblematic of our time. It's not just done, it's disseminated through social networking and blogged about by the very person who did it. He was able to create his own celebrity around it and was able to frame the conversation."*

But nearly a decade before gaining that infamy, during 2004, he was still in pursuit of that elusive fame. Eric appeared in at least two additional pornographic films; one of which was as a character named Jimmy – the name he later adopted for his male escort persona. Jimmy is also the name he used when he appeared as a pin-up model for a 2005 issue of Toronto's gay scene magazine called *FAB*. Other aliases he used in the adult film genre under include Justin, Eric Clinton Newman, Kirk Newman, Vladimir Romanov, Luka Magnotta and Rocco.

personal lives online so they would know he was watching. But soon a break would come that the group needed. In early 2012, they received a tip that he might be in Montreal. They found a photo of him online and after analyzing it, decided to track him based on landmarks in the photo. They turned to Google maps to identify the light poles in the photo that they knew would be unique to a city. Eventually they found the exact spot in Montreal where Luka had posed and felt as though they were closing in on his location.

Unbeknownst to them it came too late as Luka was sinking deeper and deeper into his dark obsession and began making numerous online posts about necrophilia and sedatives.[17] In fact, in a narrow miss, Toronto police had nearly caught up with the suspected perpetrator of the animal cruelty acts months before he committed the final deed that would launch his name being on the lips of everyone in the country. According to his former landlord in Montreal, Toronto police contacted him in March – just two weeks after Luka had already moved out of the Montreal building where he had lived for two months. At the time, Luka told his landlord he was moving back to Toronto, when he was, in fact, moving only a few kilometers away to the apartment where he would ultimately commit his infamous act.[18]

In April 2012, a video featuring numerous images of Luka was posted on the Internet asking people to help find this "serial killer". It is believed by the Animal Beta Project to have been posted by Luka himself. The video concluded with the warning "Do not approach Luka Magnotta. He is a dangerous psychopath." Ironically, that very same month, Luka underwent a one-hour psychiatric assessment with Dr. Joel Paris at the Jewish General Hospital in Montreal where he was diagnosed with Borderline Personality Disorder, a mental illness that features a pattern of impulsivity and unstable behavior. Fearing hospitalization, Luka didn't share with doctors that he was hearing voices, nor the fact that he had previously been diagnosed as a Schizophrenic. By omitting these details, he was allowed to leave the hospital without proper medical treatment.

After an 18-month investigation, the noose was tightening as the online investigators were closing in on Magnotta. The Ontario SPCA contacted the Montreal SPCA as well as police about the animal cruelty allegations. Although an Ontario SPCA representative felt

In June 2005 Eric had his first run in with the judicial system. He appeared in a Toronto court on charges of fraud and impersonation for using a woman's credit card to purchase over $16,000 worth of goods. He also faced a dozen criminal charges when police alleged he sexually assaulted a 21-year-old woman he had met online in 2004. The woman had the mental capacity of an eight-to-twelve-year-old, and while he supposedly videotaped this assault, the charge was withdrawn before the trial.[5] Lawyer Peter Skully, who represented Eric during the case, would admit years later that if Eric had been convicted of the sexual assault, it would have had a huge impact on his life as he would have been a registered sex offender and monitored, which means he would have had to report to officers who would supervise him.[6] He felt the decision to not pursue the charges would have "huge ramifications to our society eventually." Instead, Eric pled guilty to defrauding the retail stores and to impersonating the woman to get a credit card.

In a letter from Rouge Valley Medical Centre, May 2005, psychiatrist Thuraisarny Sooriabalan, stated that Eric had been diagnosed as a paranoid schizophrenic five years earlier, was receiving psychotherapy and health education, and was prescribed numerous anti-psychotic medications. However, the letter went on to say that Eric did not regularly go to the hospital to get his medications and, from the lack of medication, *"would be prone to relapse of his symptoms which include paranoia, auditory hallucinations, fear of the unknown, etc."*[7] Taking into account Eric's psychiatric issues, he spent just 16 days in jail, and the judge only issued a nine-month conditional sentence (rules to follow in order to remain out of prison) as well as just one year of probation. His community service was also reduced from 100 hours to 20 hours in view of his mental health issues. During sentencing, the judge warned him *"You have a medical problem. You need to always take medication. If you do not your life is going to get messed up."* Intuitive words – however, the judge could not have known just how "messed up" Eric's future would become.

# Reinventing Himself

**Eric Newman ceased** to exist after 2006. On August 12, he shed his birth name and legally became, Luka Rocco Magnotta. One year later, Magnotta would again appear in court; however, this time it was for a bankruptcy claim he filed in Mississauga, Ontario. Despite an elaborate online portrayal of an extravagant and glamorous life in the sex industry, he was listed as a server and reported no monthly income. His bankruptcy claim listed $17,000 in debts caused by *"illness, lack of employment and insufficient income to pay off debts."*[8]

Starting out debt free, the year 2007 saw Luka's obsession with fame lead him to audition as an underwear model for OUTtv's reality TV program COVERguy, but in the end he wasn't selected to appear on the show. He also gave a candid interview to the Naked News using the alias Jimmy, where he discussed his work as a stripper and "high end" male escort. In that same year, Luka wove an elaborate tale of his romantic involvement with high-profile serial killer Karla Homolka, who along with her husband Paul Bernardo, raped and murdered her little sister. The couple then kidnapped teenage schoolsgirls whom they enslaved, raped, tortured and killed, all while recording themselves during the crimes. (*Read more about this case in Volume 3 of the Crimes Canada series written by Peter Vronsky.*) In this extravagant hoax, Luka created Internet rumors linking himself to Homolka, and then phoned into a radio show claiming he wasn't involved with the notorious murderess. During a follow up interview with the Toronto Sun claiming he wanted to set the record straight, he not only denied knowing Homolka but also declared the rumors had ruined his life and caused him to lose modeling jobs. Asserting these so-called rumors was an ongoing conspiracy to smear his name, Luka appeared distraught during the interview, going so far as to allege death threats had been made against him. This was all a put-on, created by Magnotta to garnish media attention.

Over the ensuing years, new rumors and newspaper stories would continue to report on a link between Luka and Homolka, and someone even tried to edit her Wikipedia biography numerous times to insert Luka's name as her husband. Luka also created a tribute video to her, posing it under one of his alias YouTube accounts, but in the end these stunts did not gain him the notoriety he craved.

In February 2008, in yet another effort to make a name for himself, Luka auditioned for the reality TV show *Plastic Makes Perfect*. During the 20-minute interview, he talked about working in the adult film industry and being very comfortable in front of the camera. By that time, Luka had already undergone cosmetic surgery several times and had procedures to his eyes and nose, two hair transplant techniques, as well as surgical procedures on his teeth. He felt he was an addict but blamed it on his profession because he constantly compared himself to others and needed plastic surgery to step up his game.[9]

Luka's future cosmetic plans included pectoral and muscular implants in his biceps. But what might be the most crucial part of the interview was when Luka mentioned he had bumps on his skull that looked like devil horns. The interviewer suggested Luka could have Body Dysmorphic Disorder, and a forensic psychologist, looking back at this interview after Luka committed the murder, supported this supposition. In addition, the forensic psychologist also caught signals of serious narcissism, as well as several cases of personality disorders, saying it was not inconsistent with someone who would be considered a psychopath.[10] The *Plastic Makes Perfect* interviewer, deciding something wasn't quite right with the candidate before her, denied Luka entrance into the realm of reality television, once again dashing his hopes of using it as an avenue to attain the fame he so desperately lusted for.

Luka would fall deeper and deeper into fabricating an enormous online presence. He tried and failed to create a Wikipedia page about himself, but didn't stop there. He did successfully create the first of seventy Facebook accounts, using his many personas. He posted an article he claimed to have written called, "*How to completely disappear and never be found.*" The article was found to be largely plagiarized; however, after reading the entire post, one must ask if even then, Luka knew he may one day have to disappear.

While researching this book, it was sometimes difficult to sort fact from fiction in the world of Luka Magnotta as there is a lot of false and conflicting information on the

Internet, some of it created by Luka himself to promote his image. In June 2008, he appears to have written a post on xtube (a hardcore porn website) claiming to have had sexual intercourse with his stepmother. In an interview with the Global National, former girlfriend Nina Arsenault said Luka told her he had been routinely sexually abused as a child by an older man, and would then reenact the trauma through his work as an escort.[11] During the psychiatric assessment after his crime, he said he was repeatedly sexually assaulted by a male cousin.

Then there are his attempts at linking himself to celebrities and serial killers alike in the hope of increasing his own fame. The most well-known serial killer he tried to link himself to was, of course, Homolka. The following is a blog post, written most likely by Luka himself about their fictional relationship:

*"I was also curious about her relationship with Luka Magnotta, I was told Karla, after being released from prison was introduced to Magnotta by Richer Laponte, Luka was going to University in Montreal at the time, they became involved but quickly broke off the relationship because Karla felt too much media attention would be focused on Luka Magnotta,*

*who is a bisexual porn star. They do however remain friends, Luka now lives in Phoenix Arizona as of 2012 and goes by the name Vladimir Romanov and works in the Legal sector as a consultant, he is married and has a son with his new wife, he does keep in contact with both Lori and Karla Homolka."*[12]

However, Luka also tried to link himself to infamous serial killer Myra Hindley from Manchester, UK.[13] Hindley was an English serial killer who raped and murdered five children with Ian Brady in the 1960s, known as the Moors Murderers. In a video of himself posted to YouTube, Luka claimed to be the "Myra Hindley of Canada," and in his subsequent letter to a journalist before committing the murder, included a nod to the Moors Murder in his message.

This desperate need for fame stems from a diagnosis of the mental illness Histrionic Personality Disorder ([14]) – for which he wouldn't be diagnosed until after the homicide. Those who suffer from this condition constantly seek attention, show provocative behavior, are shallow and theatrical, and use their physical appearance to draw attention to themselves. People with Histrionic Personality Disorder often flirt and seduce others in inappropriate ways to get the attention they so desperately crave. The symptoms of this disorder seem to point to a textbook case for this man who acted in pornographic videos, supplemented his income as an escort and made up numerous stories in a bid to gain fame.

# The Dark Side of Luka Magnotta

**Tapping into his** dark side in the fall of 2010, Luka posted a link on his Facebook page called *3 guys 1 hammer,* which shows a man being violently beaten to death. He later posted conflicting information online indicating he was going to be living in places such as Los Angeles, Miami, San Diego and Moscow, Russia in an obvious effort to throw people off his track for what was to come. A few months later, shortly before Christmas, someone (later confirmed during the trial to be Luka) posted the video *1 Boy 2 Kittens* on YouTube. The Internet blew up with posts about the Vacuum Kitten Killer. The animal cruelty video shows a man with his face concealed, first playing with two kittens. He then places the kittens in a plastic bag and uses a vacuum to suck out the air and kill them. While the video was quickly removed due to policy violation, animal activists were infuriated.

The *Find the Vacuum Kitten Killer for Great Justice* Facebook Group was created and the group quickly had 4,000 people sign up.

Before the video was removed from Youtube, a copy of it was saved by the Facebook group for analysis to try to determine the identity of the person responsible. A week after the video first appeared, on December 28, 2010 animal protection group, Rescue Ink, offered a $5,000 reward for information leading to the arrest of the Vacuum Kitten Killer. The online animal activist group, The Animal Beta Project, with 11 members, then emerged. These amateur investigators interpreted the video frame by frame and allegedly linked it to Luka. A photo showed up on the Internet of Luka holding the same two cats featured in the disturbing video. Just four days later, the group received an anonymous email telling them the name of the person in the video they were desperately searching for was, in fact, Luka Magnotta, but the message listed a different background for him and said it was created in West Hollywood.[15] The group believed the email came from Luka himself trying to throw them off his track.

By this time, Luka had numerous online profiles and nearly two dozen websites under separate domain names, which listed various fabricated backgrounds including Russian mob connections, as well as simultaneous visits to

New York, Paris, Boston and Miami. Through the course of their investigation, the Animal Beta Project found that many of the images Luka posted on the Internet were, in fact, manipulated to look like he was a world traveller who visited these areas. The group did find one photo on the Internet of Luka with the GPS data intact that confirmed that Luka was actually in Toronto, Canada. The Ontario SPCA, through the urging of the online group the Animal Beta Project, opened a file on Luka Magnotta and started working with police and RCMP to find him – but to no avail. Months later, they still hadn't found Luka to answer to the allegations of animal cruelty.

By December 2011, Luka was at it again. In this second series of animal cruelty videos, he fed a live kitten to a python, and in another drowned a kitten by taping it to a broom. Trying to throw people off his track, Luka planted a story online that he had fled to Russia. Hoping to draw him out, the Animal Beta Project posted a video on their Facebook group, which featured images of Luka, listed his known aliases, and accused him as being the perpetrator in these animal cruelty cases. Their video went viral and even made the news in the United Kingdom. A story was carried in the UK

Sun, and on December 8, 2011 the UK Sun received a tip about Luka's whereabouts.

Reporter Alex West confronted Luka, and just two days later, the Sun received the following email from "John Kilbride" who was one of the victims of the Moors Murders in England by Ian Brady and Myra Hindley. At the time, it was believed to be from Luka, a speculation at the time that he later confirmed in November 2014. (**The spelling and grammatical errors are as stated in the published email**):

*Well, I have to say goodbye for now, but don't worry, in the near future you will be hearing from me again. This time, however the victims wont be small animals. I will however, send you a copy of the new video I'm going to be making. You see, killing is different than smoking... with smoking you can acutally just quit.*

*Once you kill, and taste blood, it is impossible to stop. The urge is just too strong not to continue. You have some very sexy journilists at your paper ϑ I have one I'm very keen on now. He was very sexy. You know, the fun part of all this is watching millions of people get angry and frustrated because they cant catch me. That's why I love this. I love the risk factor. Its* *so fun watching people work so hard gathering all the evidence, then not being able to name me or catch me. You see, I always win, I always hold the trump card, and I will continue to make more movies. London is wonderful because all the people are so stupid ϶ Its easy. So, I have to disappear for a while, you know… until people quit bothering me… but next time you hear from me, it will be in a movie I'm producing that will have some humans in it, not just pussys. ϶ The things I have seen and the things I have done, you can only imagine… Well, it was fun f\*\*\*\*\*\* around with everyone, so have a merry Christmas and a happy new years. I know I will. ϶ Getting away with all this, now that's genius.*

*Signed*

*Yours Truly*

*(Or is it?)*[16]

The letter clearly states the author's premeditated plan to commit a murder. Luka is certainly not the first killer in history to boast about their crimes, taking a page from the book of the likes of Jack the Ripper, the Zodiac Killer and the BTK strangler. In 1888, Jack the Ripper is believed to have sent at least three letters to the Central News Agency telling them he planned to kill again, while the Zodiac Killer who attacked couples in the San Francisco area, sent letters about the killings to a local newspaper during the 60s and 70s. The BTK (Bind, Torture, Kill) strangler killed ten people and sent his letters to police and news outlets alike between 1974 and 1991 – going so far as to suggest possible names for himself, including the one that stuck. Like these other infamous killers, Luka taunted the police to catch him. And while West notified London police that Luka was in the area after he received the letter, they said it was out of their jurisdiction, leaving Luka free to leave the United Kingdom and return to Canada.

Hoping to finally score a conviction for the animal cruelty allegations, the Animal Beta Project laid out the proof they had collected against Luka in a video, posted it online, and sent it to police – again, to no avail. While Luka had created an elaborate virtual world, in the real world Luka was practically a ghost. He had no credit cards or paper trail to follow. However, Luka knew they were on his trail and he taunted them to catch him if they could. He was tracking his trackers – going so far as to taunt them by posting details about their there was enough information provided for police to make contact, Montreal police had no file on Luka and said there was nothing they could do. Even a request from a prosecutor for a warrant was denied.[19] If they had been able to apprehend Magnotta, would it have changed the outcome? The question of "what if" will never be answered because what happened next would horrify the nation.

# A Man With A Dream

**Lin Jun, known** as Justin Lin to his friends, was born December 30, 1978. Originally from the city of Wuhan, China, he lived in a remote area of Wuhan with his family. His dream was to live in Canada to create a better life for himself and his family who, while "poor with material things" were a happy family.[20] Lin, his mother and father would all use a single bicycle to get around along bumpy village roads. Described as smart, caring, adventurous, handsome, strong, and popular by his family, Jun couldn't have known his dream of attending university in Canada, as a Chinese exchange student, would ultimately lead to his death.

He moved to Montreal in July 2011 and began attending Concordia University as an undergraduate student in engineering and computer science. His plan after graduating was to find a good job and help support his mother, father and younger sister. Despite the thousands of miles and an ocean separating them, the family remained close, communicating nearly every day. To alleviate his mother's fears about him living in a strange city so far from home, he would often walk the streets of Montreal streaming video from the area he'd settled in. But his message to her was always the same, telling her not to worry and that he was safe.[21]

A dedicated student, Jun managed his time well, and to support himself during his studies, he worked part-time at a convenience store in the tough Montreal neighborhood of Pointe-Saint-Charles. His boss described him as polite, friendly and a model employee who never missed a shift until the day of his disappearance.[22] But the immense potential of Jun would be snuffed out after his ill-fated meeting with Luka in May 2012.

# Murder, Necrophilia and Videotape

**The first reference** of the infamous *1 Lunatic 1 Ice Pick* video showed up on the Internet in the form of a photo. The image presented someone in a purple hoodie with his face concealed, holding an ice pick in front of a *Casablanca* movie poster. The image was posted on a discussion board and the ensuing posts followed the same pattern as the promotion of the previous kitten cruelty videos – the video was first promoted and then talked about under various online names on numerous websites.

On May 25 – one week after the first reference to the *1 Lunatic 1 Ice Pick* video appeared online – Jun did not show up for work. The out-of-character behavior caused his friends and mother to become worried. His friends, who had last heard from him the previous evening at 9 p.m., called his mother in China to find out if she had heard from her son. She hadn't and said she had a bad feeling. Her mother's intuition would prove to be correct.

In the online world that same day, a disturbing post showed up on the website, Ripoff Report:

*Luka Magnotta is an extremely dangerous and sick psychopath, he is incapable of feeling remorse and only thinks about how situations benefit himself. He is a sadistic, manipulative psychopath with an IQ of 145 which makes him even more dangerous. He apparently speaks three languages and is educated in Psychology and Criminal Law. He travels between Moscow, Los Angeles and New York his whereabouts are currently unknown. Psychopaths can appear very charming and look beautiful, but beware, they are cunning and highly maniacal. Luka Magnotta is a retired male model and former bisexual porn star. He is of Russian/Italian decent born in Canada. Luka Magnotta is also known for dating female serial killer Karla Homolka who murdered three girls with her husband Paul Bernardo, yet he denies these allegations.*[23]

The post goes on to detail the allegations of severe animal cruelty with a list of links to news articles and videos about the Kitten Killer – practically bragging about his previous sick acts.

Surveillance cameras captured Luka and Jun arriving together at Luka's apartment building, and on May 25 the *1 Lunatic 1 Ice Pick* video was found online, first on the Young News Channel website which features, amongst other things, images and videos of rape, murder, and animal cruelty. The video was later found on Canadian shock site Bestgore.com under the name *1 Lunatic 1 Icepick*. (Incidentally, the owner of the Bestgore.com website was later charged with one count of corrupting morals in connection with posting the video and is currently awaiting trial.) It was also found on heaven666.org named *Time to Shake Things up a Bit*.

*Warning*: **The following few pages describes the video and includes crime scene photos that are extremely graphic.**

## Murdered and Dismembered

**The ill-famed video**, which runs just over 10 minutes and has a New Order song playing as the soundtrack, begins with a man tied up, naked, a scarf over his mouth and eyes, unharmed and alive on a bed.

The soundtrack to the song True Faith starts with the lyrics:

*Something's got a hold on me*
*I get this feeling I'm in motion*
*A sudden sense of liberty*
*I don't care 'cause I'm not there*
*And I don't care if I'm here tomorrow*
*Again and again I've taken too much*
*Of the things that cost you too much*

The masked Luka sits on the victim's chest but doesn't harm him on camera. After moving the camera to the left side of the bed, you see he then walks to the side of the body and frantically stabs the torso and right arm with a screwdriver. He does so for over one minute straight with no reaction from the form on the bed. At times it appears the screwdriver is stuck on something inside the body and is hard to remove, but the crime scene is strangely clean at this point as there is no blood spray while he carries out his sick acts, proving the victim had been murdered before he started. Luka picks up the camera, walks over to the body and brings the viewer up close and personal with his handiwork thus far. He removes the scarf from Jun's face to reveal his throat has been cut and blood can be seen on the mattress where his life has drained away.

Moving down the body with the camera, he uses a serrated steak knife to make cuts on Jun's arms and legs. As the camera pans up towards Jun's head, you discover the victim has been completely decapitated and his killer picks up the severed head to roll it around, as if to add emphasis to the fact it is no longer attached to the owner's body.

In the next shot, after flipping the body over onto its stomach, it's as if you are still watching what happens next through the eyes of the killer. Holding the camera at eye level he uses a large knife to cut into the right arm near the shoulder – stopping once to zoom in on the gaping incision he has created halfway through the arm,. After making several additional cuts to

Jun's back, he eventually removes the victim's arm completely. Once the arm is free of its host, the murderer plays with the severed limb, going so far as to rub his own crotch with the hand of one of the severed arms. As if that isn't bad enough, he pulls his pants down and starts rubbing his exposed crotch with it.

Next there has been a time lapse as the killer shows a shot of what's been done to the victim – Jun is missing both arms and his right leg. While his audience is spared from these additional indignities, things are only going to get worse from here on out. The left leg, although still attached, shows a very deep incision – so much so that it's nearly cut off. He brings you in close to the wound on the right leg where the leg has been detached, and you clearly see the bone, muscle and tissue exposed. He continues sawing into the left leg, letting you watch as he continues to remove it from Jun's body.

The video jumps to a shot of the remains in full gory detail – without a head, and missing both arms and legs. With the torso turned onto its stomach on the bed, he pans in close, spreads the buttocks and places the camera beside the bed. The killer, while still clothed and hiding his face, simulates having anal sex with what is left of the body by penetrating the torso from behind (It's difficult to tell if he actually performed anal sex on the body). Just when you think it can't get any worst, he cuts out a chunk of the buttock with a knife and fork (he presumably eats it; however, this was not shown on the video).

A puppy is heard whimpering in the background and he lets the small black-and-white puppy on the bed, which gnaws on the remains of the bloody left leg stump where it has been detached from the body. (He later killed the puppy; however, this was not filmed.)

Luka further desecrates the body by using a wine bottle to penetrate the torso anally. (Note: While the video I saw didn't show this part, it came out in trial he also used a knife on the body anally.) The video then cuts to a shot of the killer laying on the bed pantless, masturbating with a severed hand, and concludes with various shots of the cut-up body around his residence – body parts in the bathtub, the decapitated head on the floor of the bathroom, a severed arm in the refrigerator, and in the final chilling image from the video is Jun with his throat slit.

Luka wasted little time in getting rid of the evidence from the crime scene – security cameras in his building which ran 24/7 caught him making several trips to the trash area in the basement of his building, and at one point he is seen wearing blue rubber gloves disposing of evidence. In addition, he was caught on camera bringing in a blue/grey suitcase, which is what he would use to dispose of the torso of Jun.

He purchased a ticket to Paris online at 4:38 a.m., scheduled to depart the next evening, and fled the country for France on May 26[24] – but not before mailing several packages.

While the video *1 Lunatic 1 Ice Pick* was reported to Toronto police and the Federal Bureau of Investigation in the United States on May 27, the video was initially dismissed as a fake. It would take three days from the time of the murder before the dismembered parts of Jun were discovered, one day after his disappearance was reported to police.

At just after 10 a.m. on May 29, police in Montreal were called to the residential building in the Côte-des-Neiges area. Janitor Mike Nadeau made the gruesome discovery of a human torso in a suitcase at 5720 Decarie in Snowdon. While he had seen the suitcase in the garbage pile the week before, he only opened it on May 29 after people complained about the smell.[25] Police would later confirm the remains belonged to Jun who had been reported missing by a close friend.

Several hours later (6 p.m.) and nearly 200 kilometres away, Prime Minister Stephen Harper's deputy chief of staff, Jenni Byrne, opened what she thought was a harmless package. Removing pink tissue paper and a black garbage bag, she uncovered a black gift bag inside. From the smell, she could tell something was wrong and immediately called police. It turned out to be a severed foot, and DNA samples later confirmed it was a missing appendage from Jun. The return address on this package, mailed to the Conservative Party, was from Logan Valentini, the name now used by Lori Homolka, sister of infamous serial killer Karla Homolka with whom Luka unsuccessfully tried to connect himself to.

Another package, this one aimed for the Liberal Headquarters in Ottawa and containing a severed hand, never reached its intended target. It was intercepted at a Canada Post facility.

Meanwhile back in Montreal, evidence collected and witness statements led officers to apartment 208 of 5720 Decarie – belonging to one Luka Magnotta. However, when the police came knocking at Luka's door, he was long gone. What remained was a message on his wall: "*If you don't like the reflection. Don't look in the mirror. I don't care.*" Inside they would find a blood-soaked mattress wrapped in plastic with duct tape and a bloody trail on the table, inside the refrigerator, the freezer and bathtub.

# Crime Scene Photos

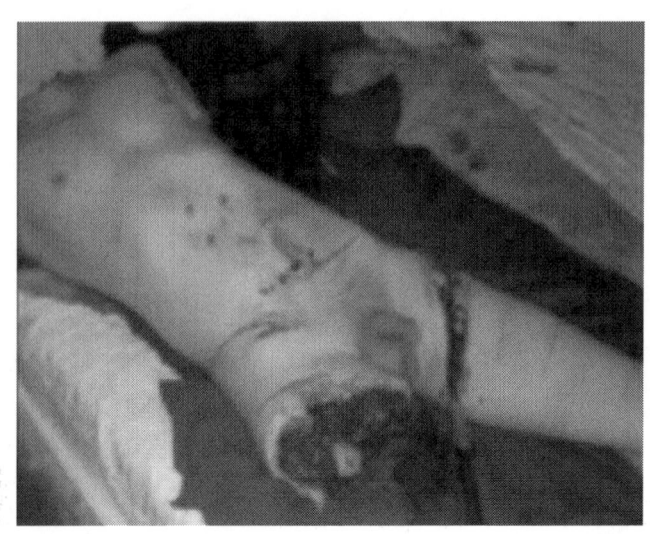

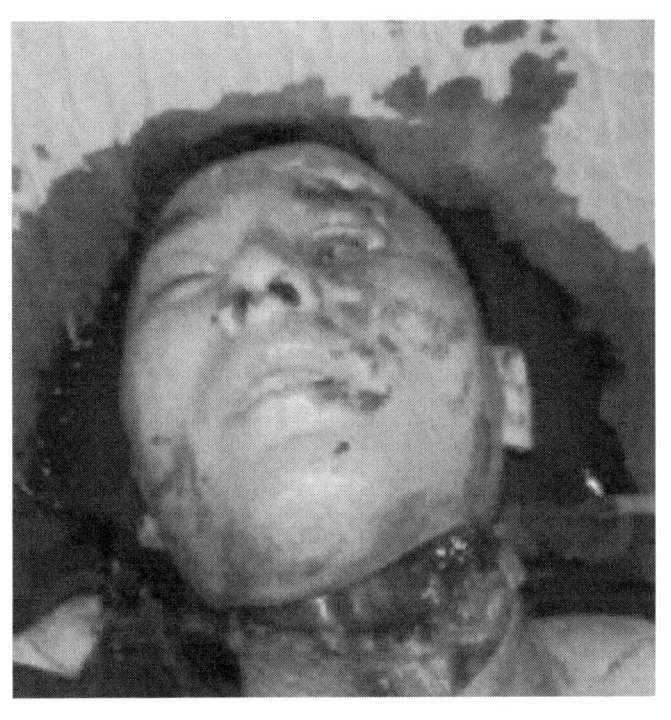

# Manhunt

**The arrest warrant** for Luka Magnotta was issued by the Service de police de la Ville de Montreal on May 30, 2012. It was upgraded to a Canada-wide warrant by the Royal Canadian Mounted Police. In the writ, Luka was accused of five counts: first-degree murder of Jun Lin; committing an indignity to the body or the human remains of Jun Lin, whether buried or not; making, printing, publishing, distributing or circulating any obscene material; making use of the mail for the purpose of transmitting or delivering anything that is obscene, indecent, immoral or scurrilous; and the final count of criminally harassing Canadian Prime Minister Stephen Harper and several (unnamed) members of Parliament.

At the same time as issuing the warrant, police were sifting through the evidence, which was quickly stacking up against Luka. They recovered several tools outside his apartment building; a pair of scissors, two knives, a screwdriver, an oscillating saw and a hammer. His second-floor bachelor apartment became a central focus of their investigation and it was there that police discovered a pink bed sheet covered in blood next to a purple, blood-streaked shower curtain. The video *1 Lunatic, 1 Ice Pick* which had originally been dismissed as a hoax was now being analyzed by police.

Interpol issued a red notice for Luka on May 31 in four official languages, Arabic, English, French and Spanish, to its 190 member countries. Montreal police told the media they were confident he fled to Europe. The next day Montreal police identified the victim in the case as Jun.

During the investigation, police were concerned they had a serial killer on their hands. Luka's online presence indicated he may have been visiting the United States around the time a similar murder took place. The Los Angeles Police Department were in contact with the Service de police de la Ville de Montreal to determine if Luka had committed the murder in that area which took place on January 17, 2012. In that instance, the severed head and hands of the victim, Hervey Medellin, were found near the Hollywood sign by two women walking their dogs.

According to one of Luka's many Facebook profiles, he was allegedly in Los Angles at the time of the murder "doing massages". The victim, who was an openly gay man, had his head, hands and feet removed from his body, indicating a similar method to the killing. The body parts were discovered in Bronson Canyon Park, near the famous Hollywood sign, suggesting the killer was seeking publicity.[26]

Police confirmed they were in contact with the LAPD to pass along relevant information from their investigation that could relate to the Hollywood Sign Murder. The animal rights group Last Chance for Animals, in the United States later claimed responsibility for creating YouTube videos that linked Luka to the murder, hoping it would draw him out while he was on the run. Last Chance for Animals created a fake YouTube account HollywoodLoveLetters as part of their investigation into Luka and posted a video called *The James Dean Killer – Luka Rocco Magnotta*, playing on Luka's interest in the movie star he said was his idol. They offered a $7,500 reward for information leading to Luka's arrest while he was on the run.

Another video they created, which referenced the Satanic Bible and described Luka as the sexiest serial killer to ever walk the earth, was designed to play to Luka's narcissistic nature. *"Taking clues from the thousands of pages of pseudonyms and online posts left by Magnotta and his many pseudonyms over the years, LCA's (Special Investigations Unit) SIU accurately predicted Magnotta would be checking websites and videos of himself from mobile devices and cyber cafes while on the run. LCA's SIU attempted to lure the killer, or his companions, using covert tactics often reserved for law enforcement and intelligence agencies."*[27]

The group claimed they even made contact with several people who could have been Luka. They turned that information over to the LAPD, but Luka was later ruled out as a suspect in the case.

The LAPD weren't the only law enforcement agencies looking to link Luka Magnotta to similar murder cases. Miami police had contacted authorities in Montreal in June 2012 regarding the 2009 death and dismemberment of Omar Laparra as they heard Luka had spent some time in their area when he was killed. In that murder case, the body parts were found floating in plastic bags in Biscayne Bay. However, no link to Luka was determined in the murder of the Guatemalan national.

Another grisly murder case in Gatineau, Quebec also gained the attention of law enforcement as they explored a connection to Luka. The body of 18-year-old Valerie Leblanc was found mutilated, burned and had severe head trauma but once again, no link was found connecting Magnotta to this homicide.

Meanwhile in Europe, and during his time on the run, police were conducting targeted searches. Magnotta was spotted in Paris by a number of people and captured on surveillance cameras at a café on June 3. There were several media reports that said he stayed in a low budget hotel in Paris, and it was during this time that he was dubbed the Butcher of Montreal by French media. Magnotta changed his appearance and travelled to Germany by bus and using the fake name Kirk Trammel[28]. The next day on June 4 at 2 p.m. Luka was discovered at an Internet café in Berlin, Germany. After being recognized and reported to police by the owner of the café, Magnotta was arrested without incident. His first words to the police, *"Ok, you got me."* Not surprisingly, at the time of his arrest, he was found looking up information about himself and watching pornography on the Internet. He was brought to a Berlin jail and the next day confirmed that he would not fight extradition back to Canada.

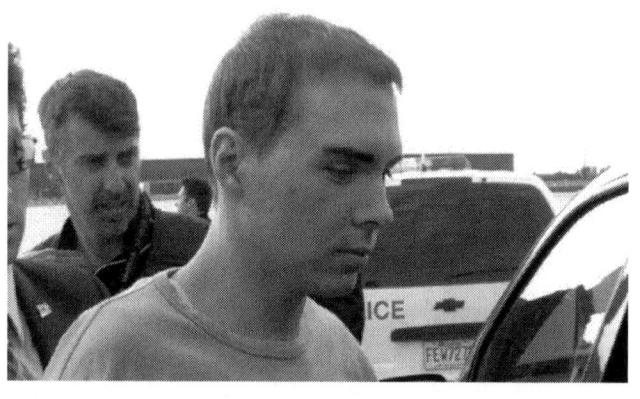

While Canadians were breathing a sigh of relief over the capture of the Butcher of Montreal, it was premature. The gruesome hold Luka held over the country wasn't over yet as on June 5, False Creek Elementary School in Vancouver opened a package containing a human hand. The return address on the package belonged to Karla Homolka's sister, Lori, who had changed her name to Logan Valentini. The note in the package, which was mailed on May 25, said: "Rose are red, violets are blue. The police will need dental records to identify you. Bitch."[29] Soon after, staff members at St. George's School in Vancouver also received a traumatizing package - this one containing a human foot. The return address for the package was for Hubert Chretien, son of Canada's former Prime Minister Jean Chretien.

Police in Montreal would confirm on June 13 that body parts in both cases belonged to Jun, and five days later Magnotta was returned to Canada to face justice for the murder.

Luka Magnotta arrived in Quebec's Mirabel International Airport under the watchful eye of several Montreal police officers via a Royal Canadian Air Force plane in a secretive extradition operation. The next day Magnotta entered a not guilty plea via satellite at a courtroom in Montreal. Two days later, he appeared briefly in person as court dates were set for a preliminary hearing for March 2013, where he requested trial by jury. Although information presented during this time is subject to a publication ban, the evidence shown caused both Luka and Jun's father to faint numerous times during the proceedings.

By this time, police had still not recovered the decapitated head of Jun, which would be retrieved from a park in Montreal on July 1 via a tip from a lawyer's office. The final piece of his remains allowed his parents to finally be able to say goodbye to their only son. On July 11, Jun's body was cremated and his ashes put to rest in a poignant 20-minute public ceremony held at Montreal's Notre-Dame-des-Neiges cemetery on July 26. Jun's family said in a statement "*We believe that Jun, carrying with him all the blessing from the society, can now rest in peace in his favorite city. The city he had chosen; Montreal.*" [30]

Surprisingly, in her eulogy, his mother forgave Magnotta for his crime and announced their charity foundation in Jun's name to help problematic youth:

*"When I first arrived in Canada, my heart was filled with sorrow and anger for my son's life being suddenly deprived. In the past two months I have been asking the same question: Canada is beautiful, its people are kind, how did this appalling tragedy happen in a peaceful society like this. Back then, I could only use 'devil' to describe the alleged murderer. But later on, when I learned more about this*

*suspect through different news sources, especially about his unfortunate upbringing, I shockingly discovered my other self who has started to develop sympathy for this person described as devil. It's true. A troubled young person may bring negative impact to the society later on when they grow up. If we can show our care for them and offer help when its needed I think we will be able to sustain a better society with love and harmony."*

While Jun's mother dreamed of sustaining a better society through love, Luka's despicable actions garnered the wrong kind of love through a legion of admirers. As is the case with many notorious killers, Magnotta developed a large following of obsessed fans after his capture by police, further catering to his need for attention.

Commonly known as groupies, they idolized the infamous killer and exhibited little regard for the feeling of Jun's family. As RJ Parker discusses in his book, *Serial Killer Groupies*, many of these groupies suffer from hybristophilia – a *"paraphilia of the predatory type in which a person can be sexually aroused, or even achieve orgasm in response to, or contingent upon, being with a partner who is known to have committed an outrage, like cheating or lying or known infidelities of crime, such as rape, murder or armed robbery."*

Known commonly as the Bonnie and Clyde Syndrome, mental health experts said one reason many women feel affectionate towards serial killers is because they suffer from an extreme form of fanaticism. Other psychologists believe their interest stems from the fact that killers are "alpha males – powerful, lethal and are able to break the rules – and, as a result, they are able to easily attract women" due largely to the fact that throughout history men who were able to protect their women and children were considered desirable.

While Magnotta doesn't meet the standard definition of a serial killer as he only committed one murder, the potential was there for him to become one if he hadn't been apprehended. Even so, he developed a loyal fan base of men and women (in large part women) who showed their support online and by writing to him in the prison.

One of the defunct Facebook pages run by administrator Tiffiee Da KittyLad said *"We may not be \*\*fans\*\* of what he did, but I believe in him as a person, and loved him* *before all this happened,*" while another Facebook group set up by Allyssa Kerr is "*for people who are fastiated [sic] with Luka, or anything that goes against society, and their morals, or who would just want to have sex with him.*" What is surprising and disturbing is that some said they found Luka's *1 Lunatic 1 Ice Pick* video to be "inspirational."

Destiney St. Denis of Saskatoon was the administrator for the Facebook group Support Luka Magnotta which had over 1,400 members before being taken down for inappropriate content. She said in an email to the National Post "*I like Luka Magnotta because he is inspirational, nice, and very very good looking. I have seen the video over 20 times. I do think that was him, and I liked it. He is inspirational because he is not afraid of himself.*" St. Denis had made contact with Luka during the kitten killer controversy, long before Jun's murder. They became virtual friends and would chat on Skype twice a week before the murder. After his capture, she had planned to visit him in prison.[31]

She admitted she is unapologetic to the feelings of victim's family, astonishingly adding: "*I think that if anyone is a victim in this case, it is Luka ... because all the bullying that he had to endure prior to the murders. I've seen worse in horror films. I really like horror films. He's a very nice person. We talked a lot about fashion design."*

Others recognize that it is not normal to be obsessed with someone who had committed such a horrific act. Such is the case for one supporter, Lexa Mancini, who runs the blog Luka Magnotta Obsession, *"I'm aware that there is some cognitive dissonance involved in supporting Luka the way I do. It's just impossible to reconcile the beauty and the beast within him. On the one hand, I adore this image he has created for himself, even though I'm fully aware it is not real. As has been pointed out, his surgically altered face is not even real, but this just doesn't make him any less attractive."*[32] She said her husband, who is aware of her self-described "school-girl crush" on the murderer, suggested she see a psychologist. *"It's like we're all a part of a reality TV show directed by none other than Luka himself,"* she wrote on her blog. *"Only it's not reality. Half of this obsession takes place in our own heads, thinking about Luka, daydreaming of conversations we might have with him."*

# The Fame Monster

**When news of** the murder broke, the media questioned what could make someone commit such a horrific act, calling in numerous experts and profilers for interviews. The shocking nature of the crime guaranteed extensive media coverage. He had finally got what he wanted – his name was on the lips of nearly everyone in the country. Media outlets tried to learn as much as possible about Luka Magnotta, and there certainly was a lot online to sift through.

Luka was named Canada's 2012 Newsmaker of the Year by the Canadian Press. It was a controversial move – one many people expressed outrage over. However, some criminal psychologists actually credited the media in aiding in the capture of Luka before he could commit another murder.

As you could suspect in a cast like this, the media was flooded with reports about "The Canadian Psycho" and psychologists were also lining up to give their insights on what could drive someone to commit such despicable acts.

In a Toronto Sun interview, Oren Amitay, a Toronto psychologist and lecturer at Ryerson University, said in the June 9, 2012 article that some people are just born evil and that Luka may fall into that category. He said the animal torture allegations point to signs of him being a psychopath. *"And on top of that, he's a narcissistic or histrionic psychopath – in that he wants everyone to know who he is... Most people who have anti-social personality, who also hurt animals as children don't go onto killing people. I'm not sure what made him cross that line."* [33] Amitay also said a lot of times there's a ritual involved for psychopaths and serial killers and, for Luka, taking pictures was part of that ritual.

The article also went on to quote an unnamed family member who described Luka as a ticking time bomb and a nut job who had delusions of grandeur, concocting stories that eventually became fact in his mind.

Mary Ellen O'Toole, a retired senior criminal profiler for the Federal Bureau of Investigation, who has seen cases such as the Zodiac Killer, the Unabomber and the Green River Killer, gave her expert opinion based on Luka's past behavior. She said sending Lin's body parts in the mail accomplished two things: to degrade the victim and to shock people. She reasoned that his actions of recording their own activities could be part of sexual sadism where individuals with that parasitic behavior become sexually aroused by the victim's response to the affliction.

Criminologist and behavioral analyst Dr. Casey Jordan weighed in on his actions while Magnotta was still on the run, and she said in an interview with the Sun News that his lack of a conscience wouldn't have happened overnight. *"This would be the product of a very dysfunctional childhood. To be honest, if the allegations of the kitten abuse, which go back two or three years, are the first time he tortured animals I would be very surprised. Usually animal torture or picking on anyone more vulnerable than he is would have manifested itself perhaps in the teenage years. But we do know that if he is morphing from sociopathic or a lack of ability to feel any empathy, or badness for other people, he could be transforming into psychosis, having delusions because clearly he is out of touch with reality."*

She said if you want to think of it as a spectrum or actual trajectory that he was moving along, it manifested several years ago in animal torture, to the point he was actually bragging online that he could not only make himself disappear, but that his sexual aberrations were misunderstood and unpopular.

*"The warning signs have been there all along. To be honest 99 per cent of the time it's all just bravado, they don't really act on it. In his particular case, he planned this. He acted on it. He mailed those body parts and he had an escape plan already figured out. Now that is very frightening because he is also known to have said that he will kill again."*[34]

After his capture, in a separate interview, Dr. Jordan felt the media exposure of the crime contributed to Luka's capture before he could act again. There is a careful balance media have to observe when covering these cases. She felt that the coverage of the murder wasn't for sensationalistic purposes but the quality of this crime was so off the charts with regards to the seriousness and the aberration of it, the attention it received put his face in the public and appears to be directly responsible for how he got apprehended. However, had that attention waned, she felt he would have killed again.

*"I believe he is so addicted to the attention seeking disorder that if the media had quit paying any attention to him, if there was no international manhunt, I do think he was at high risk for doing something again just for the sole purpose of getting the media attention back on him."* [35]

Another case that drew massive media attention was that of Mark Twitchell, a Canadian convicted of murder in 2011 for the online luring death of John Altinger. Many people in North America compared Luka's case to Twitchell's, because they both documented their crimes and heavily used social media in the planning and execution of these murders.

Twitchell's crime was inspired by the Dexter novels and television series, which features the main character Dexter Morgan, a serial killer who works as a forensic bloodstain pattern analyst for the Miami Metro Police Department. Luka's crime parallels connections to several movies. In his letter to media six months before committing the murder, he quoted lines from the movie Basic Instinct; on the murder video he was shown stabbing Jun's body multiple times with an icepick – the murder weapon of choice in Basic Instinct; and when fleeing the country, he traveled in Europe under the name Trammel – the last name of the character Sharon Stone played in the very same movie. Luka's act of mailing his victim's body parts is reminiscent of the movie Se7en which starred Brad Pitt and Morgan Freeman as detectives hunting for a deranged serial killer; and finally, the murder video he posted online used the soundtrack from the movie American Psycho. It is interesting to note that the prosecution even wanted the jury to watch the movie Basic Instinct as part of the trial, but the motion was denied.[36]

Journalist Steve Lillebuen, who published a book about the Twitchell case, wrote an interesting article for CNN about the public's sick fascination with Jun's death after the news broke about the video Luka had created. In it, Lillebuen discusses how people share pretty much everything online, where it is no longer the norm to keep offensive material hidden in the deep Web. Essentially, Luka's video exposed the underbelly of the Internet and pushed it into wide circulation – bringing people from passive viewers of a crime to being a participant.

*"Our fascination with the macabre has always been there, but are we becoming desensitized to such violence when it transforms from fiction into the real thing?"* wrote Lillebuen. *"With every click of this video, it's as if we've gone from wanting to be a fly on the wall of a crime scene to being a fly on the corpse. Responsible journalists, who aim to find balance and sensitivity when reporting on serious crimes by adding context, holding back or blurring the most offensive parts, have been pushed aside by this crowd of gross-out seekers."*[37]

As seen with the Twitchell and Luka cases, with the invention of social media, the medium used for murderers to share their messages and criminal activities is easily accessible. From vandalism to sexual abuse to murder, perpetrators are confessing and bragging about acts on the Internet.[38] You have to wonder where did society go wrong? When did we become so desensitized to violence that it became okay to share with your friends and acquaintances a despicable video like the one Luka created.

And while you can use words like sick, disturbing and gruesome to describe what Luka did to Jun, what is the most disturbing thing is that he was never diagnosed as a psychopath or a sociopath. Instead his diagnosis would include borderline personality disorder, histrionic personality disorder, paranoid schizophrenia, and psychosis, along with some narcissistic and antisocial traits. However, some people strongly suspected Luka Magnotta was pretending to be schizophrenic in the hope of lending credibility to his defense against the murder charges.

# The Trial

**The trial of** Luka Magnotta began on September 8, 2014 with jury selection that spanned eight days. There were 1,600 prospective jurors with 12 bilingual jurors and two bilingual alternates selected. The difficulty in choosing an impartial jury was attributed to the media coverage and infamy surrounding the crime. All of the arguments for the trial were expected to take six to eight weeks. Ultimately the trial was held in a high security courtroom, with the defendant housed behind a thick, protective glass, and a publication ban was in place for media.

The opening day of Luka's trial on September 29 featured what can only be described as a stunning revelation; Luka admitted to the murder of Jun; however, he pled not guilty to all five charges brought against him. Using what was previously known as the insanity defense but is now called NCR for not criminally responsible, Luka's lawyer, Luc Leclair, said in his opening remarks that while Luka committed the acts, he should not be held responsible because of his mental state. The prosecutor, on the other hand, argued that Luka not only knew what he was doing, but that the murder was planned months in advance.

Quebec Superior Court Judge Guy Cournoyer told jurors it was up to them to determine if Luka was of sound mind during the murder. Taking the stand for the defense during the trial would be some of Luka's family, including his father, who would report on their family's history with mental illness, as well as several physicians who had treated Luka in the past.

Forensic investigator Caroline Simoneau was the Crown's first witness in the case. She presented numerous photographs taken from the scene and around the apartment building where the crime took place, including those of the locked suitcase containing Jun's torso. Inside one garbage bag was a part of a leg wrapped in other garbage bags, in another was a small, black dead dog, and a third held even more human body parts. Surveillance tapes from the five cameras that ran twenty-four hours a day at Luka's apartment building were entered into evidence during the trial and provided a timeline of the hours and days that passed from the time Jun innocently walked into the building with Luka, never knowing he wouldn't leave the building alive.

After committing the murder, Magnotta is shown acting calmly, in different outfits, leaving and entering the building multiple times, each time carrying a trash bag, and each time he would pause to look at himself in the lobby's mirror. It appeared at one time he was wearing the same yellow t-shirt Jun wore when he arrived. Another recording was that of the delivery of a pizza he ordered while cleaning up the evidence. During a timeframe of approximately two hours, Luka was caught on camera repeatedly going to the basement to dispose of items in the garbage bins – disposing of full garbage bags stretched from the weight of their contents, filled with clothing, etc.[39]

The jury also heard how the police initially thought the torso found in the suitcase belonged to Magnotta because a piece of paper was found with, "Luka Rocco Magnotta 1982/07/24" written on it. However, once the grotesque snuff film was brought to the officer's attention, that theory changed and Luka became the prime suspect. In addition, they found several items featured in the film while picking through the mound of garbage – a Casablanca poster and the wine bottle used in the video.

The four hand-written notes on small pieces of paper that accompanied the dismembered body parts sent through the postal service were also brought to light. The note accompanying the package addressed to the Conservative Party headquarters said: *"Stephen Harper and Lauren [sic] Teskey will know who this is. They fucked up big time."* Teskey is the maiden name of Prime Minister Stephen Harper's wife. The note to the Liberal Party which, as mentioned earlier, never made it to its intended target as it was intercepted at a postal processing centre, said *"You need to talk to Lauren Teskey and her family! Lots to hide!"*

Each of the packages mailed by Luka had a different return name and address including one bearing the name L.Valentini, the name used by Karla Homolka's younger sister, as well as Hubert Chretien – the former Prime Minister's son. Both testified during the trial, and Lori's testimony would expose a shocking revelation – her infamous sister was living in Canada again. However, that wasn't the only link to Karla. The other two boxes had the name Bordelais on the return address section.[40]

Bordelais is believed to be a nod to Karla Homolka who married Thierry Bordelais, the brother of her former Quebec lawyer. Karla was at one time found living under the name Leanne Bordelais.

The autopsy report presented at trial noted the likely cause of death was the long cut along the victim's neck. Of the fifty-five stab wounds to the body, thirty-seven were to the upper body and eighteen to the abdomen. Although Jun was already dead, some of the cuts were deep enough to puncture his lungs and intestines. Seventy-three superficial cuts were cataloged on Lin's back, arms and legs, while part of his buttocks was cut out. There were so many blunt force traumas to the skull, likely from a hammer, that the pathologist couldn't count them all. There were no signs of defensive wounds, and the body was dismembered after his death had occurred. A toxicology report had detected some level of sleeping pills and allergy medication in Lin's system. As well, the tips of the fingers on one hand were damaged, which may have indicated his killer tried to remove his fingerprints.

Testimony was heard regarding the camera discovered in the garbage outside

Luka's apartment. While the camera could not be turned on, police were able to recover 15 videos and 505 photographs on the camera's memory card. The raw files found on this camera were used to make the 10-minute video posted online. The raw footage played during the trial subjected the jurors to the sounds from the apartment, including that of the numerous stab wounds inflicted to Jun. The video also reveals his throat was slashed before these stabbings took place.

After forty-eight witnesses, the prosecution rested its case on October 31, 2014.

Luka chose not to testify during the trial. While mounting his defense, a number of doctors and psychiatrists were called to the stand. The court heard that, prior to 2003, Luka had been diagnosed as manic depressive and mildly schizophrenic. Dr. Allan Tan treated Luka in Toronto between 2003 and 2009, and testified that his patient did admit to hearing voices in 2004. In 2005, Luka told his doctor he was convinced he was being stalked and watched, and that voices in his head told him to walk like an ape. In addition he reported that people were taking pictures of him and posting them online to ruin his modeling career.

Dr. Thomas Barth, the German psychiatrist who met with Luka daily in a Berlin prison hospital for a week after his arrest, testified that he believed Luka suffered a "severe psychotic episode related to suspected paranoid schizophrenia."[41] During their meetings, Luka claimed he had a 35-year-old American ex-boyfriend named Manny who was a pimp. This boyfriend allegedly forced Luka to have sex with other men, beat him, and forced him to make bestiality sex tapes. Luka also claimed he was being watched and filmed by a witch named Debbie; alleged his ex-boyfriend Robin tried to poison him and forced him to take steroids; and he told Barth he always felt handicapped because of his schizophrenic father and that he hated his alcoholic mother. [42]The prosecutor, upon cross-examination, questioned if Luka's ramblings were measured to have on file for his eventual defense.

In Dr. Marie-Frederique Allard's[43] testimony, she said when Luka recounted for the first time his version of the murder of Jun, he was "anxious, ill and breathing arduously." While police were never able to determine how Jun and Luka met, Luka claimed to Allard that Jun responded to his May 23 post on Craigslist for a sexual partner interested in bondage. In his version of events, they met at a metro station the following day and then went to Luka's apartment where they drank wine, talked and had sex. During her testimony, Dr. Allard said Luka told her he was the first to be tied to the bed but that he was experiencing pain and asked Jun to stop once he gave Luka "small hits" on the back of the head. Luka put some tablets of Temazepam in his own wine glass and alleges Jun asked for some as well – dispensing two or three tablets at his request. When Luka went to the window and noticed a black car outside, Luka told Allard he became convinced Jun was a government agent sent to kill him. These voices in his head were talking and laughing, telling him to tie up Jun and "cut it" and to "Do it, he's from the government." Luka then told Allard he slit Jun's throat, and the voices said to "stab it, stab it" while he was standing over the body. He told her these same voices told him to kill his puppy.

Based on the twenty-five hours Dr. Allard examined Luka, she told the court his schizophrenic illness was to blame the night he committed the murder and that he couldn't distinguish between right and wrong. She told the court about his medical history, that he had stopped taking his prescribed medication the summer before moving to Montreal, and Luka believed people were following him, people were teasing him, and that he was being watched by the government. It was her belief that the voices in his head telling Luka to "give it back, give it back," meant he should return the body to the government – leading him to send the packages to the Liberal and Conservative parties. Luka told her he posted the video online in an attempt to stop the voices in his head and he left the country because he had already made the plan to move to Paris.

During cross examination of her testimony, the prosecutor pointed out that Luka had a history of withholding critical medical information and even lying to doctors, so it reasons that he could be lying to avoid a jail sentence. Dr. Allard said lots of people lie and admitted it was difficult to tell when Luka was being truthful. However, she maintained that his actions were attributed to his illness.

Luka had presented a slightly different version of events to Dr. Joel Watts, who diagnosed Luka with paranoid schizophrenia, psychosis, and borderline personality disorder with histrionic traits. The defense once again brought up a man named Manny, an American from New Mexico who Luka says he met while living in New York City through his job as an escort in 2010. Manny would have a starring role in the 124-page forensic Psychiatry Evaluation submitted to the court by Dr. Watts for the defence.

In it he explained that Manny tried to convince Luka that his medication would make him suicidal and that he became abusive when Luka wanted to stay on his meds. Despite telling Dr. Watts that he was fearful of Manny, Luka continued to see him and recounted one instance where Manny wanted a threesome where they did sexual acts that were embarrassing, including urination. Manny apparently filmed this encounter and suggested Luka could make more money than he was at that time if they made more videos – including "crush" videos (where women sit on rabbits) that featured kittens as the animal of choice.

Luka also told Dr. Watts that Manny insisted he make this animal cruelty video, showed him where to set up the camera, and took pictures of him having "sex with them, rubbing myself with them." Manny then took the memory card and posted the video on the Internet. In Luka's mind, Manny was also to blame for the subsequent animal cruelty video where he fed one cat to a python and drowned the second by taping it to a broom.

The report chronicles that Manny had *"forced him to drink alcohol, smoke marijuana, that he had strangled him, bit him, cut him with a knife, punched him with his keys, forced him to drink his own urine and eat his feces, spit on him and told him that if he went to any doctors he would kill him. He alleged Manny forced him to eat animal parts, to have sex with his puppy and numerous cats, and that he had raped him and performed several humiliating and degrading sex acts on him against his will. He verbally insulted him and had killed one of his cats by stepping on its head."*

Luka described Manny to Dr. Watts as "an abusive tormentor who allegedly forced him to stop taking his anti-psychotic medications and to film video in which cats were killed."[44] Police had not been able to corroborate Manny's existence, but Dr. Watts, in his testimony, said that while he believes Manny does exist, many of Luka's experiences with Manny were hallucinatory as he admitted to hearing Manny at times when he couldn't see him.

As with the case of Luka's previous illegal activity, during the night of the murder, Manny was once again present. According to the psychiatric assessment, Manny told Luka that Jun had possibly drugged him and could have been an agent working for the government. Luka told Dr. Watts it was Manny who told him to kill Jun.

*"I felt I did not have control of my body, something was controlling me. I was hearing different voices that I could not understand, almost like a radio between stations and my head was going fast. I thought he was an agent, that he was going to hurt me. [sic] My mind started racing very fast. I don't remember what was happening. It was like a blackout. I remember feeling wet, hearing (voice) saying 'cut it'."*

Luka said he remembers feeling sick and throwing up, but not much besides that. *"I remember bits and pieces, waking up, I don't remember what was happening. I just blocked all this out."* Manny was still in his head telling him he would handle everything, and Luka said he did not remember dismembering Jun, mailing the body parts, nor his comings and goings the next day.

While Luka did not recall his reasoning for hiding Lin's head in a park, he said he had wanted to tell police where the head was because he didn't want Jun's mother to suffer as he knew *"it was important to her peace of mind."*(sic) He did recall he brought Lin's head to the park to do a religious ceremony on it and saying the words "May God rest on your soul." He also said he may have made a makeshift cross to put with Lin's head.

On November 25, 2014, after hearing from twelve witnesses, the defense rested its case. On December 4, the jury heard from six rebuttal witnesses bringing the total number of witnesses during the entire trial to sixty-six during the forty-day trial. During his closing arguments, defense attorney Luc Leclair told jurors "insanity is insanity". The prosecution however, said in its address that Luka was "purposeful, mindful, ultra-organized and ultimately responsible for his actions."[45]

# Verdict

**At the conclusion** of the trial, the jury, which deliberated for eight days, delivered a guilty verdict for each of the five counts on Tuesday, December 23, 2014. The murder conviction alone carries a life imprisonment sentence with no chance of parole for 25 years. He was given the maximum sentence for the four other charges, receiving an additional 19 years to be served concurrently.

On Monday, January 19, Luka filed two appeals of his conviction of the murder of Jun and requested a new trial. The first appeal cited a number of judicial errors while the other featured a number of other issues. The appeal hearing was scheduled to take place in Montreal on Feb 18, 2015. However, when February 18 came, Luka instead withdrew both of his appeals of the first-degree murder of Lin Jun. [46]

Jun's family remained relatively quiet during the entire proceedings, releasing a select few statements to media.

After his death, Jun's family described

their beloved son as their pride and hope. "Jun Lin believed in Buddhism. He was very kind and always enjoyed helping others. To his parents, he was a loving and considerate son. To his sister, he was a big brother who was always there for her... His friends said he was optimistic, ambitious and open-minded. He always trusted people with a positive approach to life."[47] That trust was misplaced and would cost him his life in a low-rent apartment in Montreal.

Canadians rallied around Jun's family, offering their support in various ways throughout the ordeal. Through Concordia University, money was raised to help with the expenses incurred while they were seeking justice for their son. The tragedy united individuals from across the globe, and the family said they were comforted by the knowledge their son's name will live on in a positive light through the Jun Lin Family Fund, which will provide financial assistance for Chinese students studying at Concordia University.

After the trial, Jun's father released a heart-wrenching victim impact statement, which truly brings home the effect this situation has had on their family.

While this book chronicles how Luka

Magnotta became known as the Cannibal Porn Star, I wanted to end this book with the words from Jun's family because sometimes it's easy to forget about the victim in such a sensational case. That would be a disservice to the man whose life ended too soon and his family who will forever by haunted by Luka.

# Victim's Impact Statement

*I do not know who I am supposed to be talking to, who will listen to this or read this but I do need to say something. For me, for Lin Jun's mother, for Lin Jun's sister.*

*My brave son, smart son, laughing son, caring son, adventurous son, handsome son, strong son, popular son. Gone. And I will always miss you Lin Jun.*

*The night Lin Jun died, parts of many other people died in one way or another. His mother, his sister and me, his friends, Lin Feng. In one night, we lost a lifetime of hope, our futures, parts of our past.*

*I have trouble thinking of other things, to concentrate. Lin Jun's mother is not right anymore, has not smiled or laughed much since May 2012 and will never work again. Lin Jun's sister has tried to take care of her mother but she too is unable to work, is sad. She has too much responsibilities now for someone so young. I hope one day she is better.*

*My memories of Lin Jun do not stop at his youth but now I see those memories through his death, how he died, how he must have suffered, how humiliating his death has become with a movie, post office packages, and only the accused's story that it was not his fault and the fault of government agents.*

*I know that the accused is not what Canada is about. Lin Jun loved China but was also drawn to Canada, to live in Montreal, in French. I have spent now more time in Canada and now know why my son wanted to live here. This knowledge hurts all the more to know what my son is missing by not being alive in your country. I am troubled by knowing what his plans were, to stay here and to start a business, to live here permanently, to enjoy your language, your opportunities, your fresh air. I live each day with regret that all I now see available here will never be his, that his name will only be associated with a horrible, degrading crime.*

*It causes me fresh pain to know that my son's legacy is to be remembered as a victim. He not only suffered in his murder but will be humiliated for each time his name is mentioned and it hurts me deeply and will hurt me forever. It hurts me to know that my last words to him were "be careful son." I feel bad that I was not there to warn him that night. I will never see his smiling face on video chat or hear about his new accomplishments or hear his laugh. Lin Jun's birthday is on December 30 and he will never be there for his birthday or ours.*

*In traditional Chinese culture, your child grows up to take care of you when you get old. A Chinese parent has a saying : " 养儿防老 " (Yang (3) er(2) fang(2) lao(3)). "Having a child takes care of old age" or "Raising a child prevents loneliness in old age". He will not be there for me and Lin Jun's mother in our old age. I turned sixty years old at the start of the trial and so did Lin Jun's mother a few days later. We have only misery as a gift and feel pain for his little sister Mei Mei. I thought I would be able to retire and enjoy my son being there for me, with me, to let me feel I have been a good father. His chair is empty at my home. His phone never answers. All gone. I have no ability or desire to want anything else.*

*I am told that the accused will receive the maximum under Canadian judicial system for one of his crimes. I appreciate the result. I am told that a prisoner in Canada is given time to reflect on his crime, to live with the bad memor-*

*ies, to perhaps feel regret, to be cut off from family, to be limited in their movements. In that understanding, I think that his future sounds like mine, Lin Jun's mother's and Lin Jun's sister. We are cut off from our son, and given the rest of our lives to think. We reflect on that crime, we feel regret, we have no desire to go anywhere or see people.*

*I am also told that for the next years, a prisoner will be housed, his bed provided, his food prepared, doctors made available and psychiatrists to listen to him and give him medication when he tells them that he feels bad.*

*No one will house us, feed us or provide doctors. Lin Jun will never be there for us. We do not want to tell our story because it is too sad to repeat. We cannot talk much about Lin Jun without talking about his murder. The murder has robbed us not only of Lin Jun but our ability to think and talk about him without feeling pain and shame.*

*I had come to see your trial system to see justice done and I leave satisfied that you have not let my son down.*

*I had come to learn what happened to my son*

*that night and I leave without a true or a complete answer.*

*I had come to see remorse, to hear some form of apology, and I leave without anything.*

*– Lin Diran[48]*

# Acknowledgements

*Thank you to my editor and proof-readers for your support:*

## -- Cara Lee

Bettye McKee

Lorrie Suzanne Phillippe

Marlene Fabregas

Darlene Horn

Ron Steed

June Julie Dechman

Katherine McCarthy

Robyn MacEachern

Charlotte Ellis

# Other Books in Crimes Canada

1. *Robert Pickton: The Pig Farmer Killer* by CL Swinney (March 2015)

2. *Marc Lepine: The Montreal Massacre* by RJ Parker (April 2015)

3. *Paul Bernardo and Karla Homolka: The Ken and Barbie Killers* by Peter Vronsky (May 2015)

4. *Shirley Turner: Doctor, Stalker, Murderer* by Kelly Banaski (June 2015)

*Crimes Canada Web Page*

***www.CRIMESCANADA.com***

# About the Author

**Cara Lee Carter** is an award-winning journalist and experienced communications professional with nearly a decade of experience in marketing, communications and social media management for which she has won numerous national and international awards in these areas, including writing.

Born and raised in Newfoundland and Labrador, Canada, Cara Lee discovered her love of story telling at an early age and began her first internship at a daily newspaper while still in high school. Trained as a journalist, it was an easy move to the field of marketing and communications where she remains today. The world of true crime writing was a logical leap for this self-professed book junkie, and she's excited to launch her first book under the tutelage of internationally acclaimed authors, RJ Parker and Peter Vronsky.

# Contact Information

### Email -

*AuthorCaraLeeCarter@gmail.com*

### Facebook -
*https://www.facebook.com/authorcaraleecarter*

### Amazon Author Page -

*http://rjpp.ca/Amazon-CaraLeeCarter*

### Publisher's Author Page -

*rjpp.ca/CaraLeeCarter*

### Website -

*http://www.CaraLeeCarter.com/*

*Thank you for purchasing and reading my debut book. It would be greatly appreciated if you would write a brief review on the site where you obtained this book.*

*Thanks so much, Cara Lee*

# Table of Contents

Copyrights..................................................................................3
Crimes Canada: True Crimes That Shocked the Nation Series Introduction..................................................................................5
Birth or Making of a Psychopath?............................................9
    Nature......................................................................................13

    Nurture....................................................................................16

Background..............................................................................19
The Early Years........................................................................23
Drunk on Ego...........................................................................29
Reinventing Himself................................................................35
The Dark Side of Luka Magnotta...........................................43
A Man With A Dream.............................................................53
Murder, Necrophilia and Videotape.......................................57
Murdered and Dismembered..................................................61
Crime Scene Photos.................................................................68
Manhunt....................................................................................73
The Fame Monster...................................................................85
The Trial....................................................................................93
Verdict.....................................................................................107
Victim's Impact Statement....................................................111
Acknowledgements................................................................117
Other Books in Crimes Canada.............................................119
About the Author...................................................................121
    Contact Information............................................................123

Citations..................................................................................126

# Citations

[1] http://montrealgazette.com/news/local-news/psychiatrists-report-chronicles-the-making-of-luka-magnotta

[2] http://montrealgazette.com/news/local-news/psychiatrists-report-chronicles-the-making-of-luka-magnotta

[3] http://globalnews.ca/news/1714436/tracing-luka-magnottas-footsteps-the-making-of-a-killer/

[4] http://www.youtube.com/watch?v=DsQbaET604g

[5] http://www.theglobeandmail.com/news/national/new-light-shed-on-luka-magnottas-mental-health-shows-he-was-diagnosed-with-schizophrenia/article10713680/

[6] http://www.youtube.com/watch?v=Vyb4fOBMWds

[7] http://globalnews.ca/news/451660/magnotta-diagnosed-with-paranoid-schizophrenia-2005-doctors-letter-reveals/

[8] http://www.ottawacitizen.com/Magnotta+bankruptcy+filing+reveals+life+lacking+glamour/6727134/story.html

[9] www.youtube.com/watch?v=Cn1v3btU3tU

[10] http://www.youtube.com/watch?v=1IPRK6Fjpao

[11] http://www.youtube.com/watch?v=1IPRK6Fjpao

[12] http://thierry-karla-homolka-luka-magnotta-2.blogspot.ca/2011/11/karla-homolka-emily-bordelais-luka.html

[13] http://abproject.org/docs/Kitten%20Killer%202010%20-%202011.pdf

[14] http://psychcentral.com/disorders/histrionic-personality-disorder-symptoms/

[15] http://www.youtube.com/watch?v=Vyb4fOBMWds

[16] http://magnottafiles.blogspot.ca/p/timeline.html

[17] http://www.cbc.ca/news2/interactives/magnotta-luka/

[18] http://www.huffingtonpost.ca/2012/06/24/luka-rocco-magnotta-landlord_n_1622604.html

[19] http://www.youtube.com/watch?v=Vyb4fOBMWds

[20] http://www.huffingtonpost.ca/2012/07/16/jun-lin-mother-interview_n_1677814.html

[21] http://www.youtube.com/watch?v=Vyb4fOBMWds

[22] http://www.citynews.ca/2012/06/01/victim-jun-lin-hadnt-missed-a-shift-until-disappearance-boss/

[23] http://www.ripoffreport.com/r/Luka-Magnotta-Bisexual-Male-Model-and-Porn-Actor/New-York-New-York-10001/Luka-Magnotta-Bisexual-Male-Model-and-Porn-Actor-Luka-Magnotta-Male-Model-Luka-Magnotta-Ma-887359

[24] "Serial Killer Groupies", RJ Parker, December 2014. 265 pages ISBN:13- 978-1502540904

[25] http://www.cbc.ca/news/canada/montreal/torso-found-in-montreal-garbage-pile-1.1280480

[26] http://observer.com/2012/06/lapd-investigating-connection-between-luka-magnotta-and-hollywood-sign-killing/

[27] http://www.marketwired.com/press-release/lca-takes-cutting-edge-investigation-accused-murderer-animal-abuser-luka-magnotta-1665809.htm

[28] "Serial Killer Groupies", RJ Parker, December 2014. 265 pages ISBN:13- 978-1502540904

[29] http://www.thepost.on.ca/2014/10/17/luka-magnotta-trial-to-hear-from-new-witnesses

[30] http://www.cbc.ca/news/canada/jun-lin-s-mother-has-sympathy-for-alleged-killer-1.1181496

[31] http://www.huffingtonpost.ca/2012/07/09/luka-rocco-magnotta-fans-facebook-blog_n_1658533.html

[32] http://www.huffingtonpost.com/2012/07/13/luka-magnotta-accused-cannibal-female-fans_n_1668129.html

[33] http://www.torontosun.com/2012/06/09/was-luka-magnotta-born-evil

[34] http://www.calgarysun.com/videos/1667942193001#1667942252001

[35] http://www.calgarysun.com/videos/1667942193001#1672950373001

[36] http://www.macleans.ca/society/technology/why-magnottas-motive-is-almost-as-disturbing-as-what-he-did/

[37] http://edition.cnn.com/2012/06/06/opinion/lillebuen-killing-video/index.html

[38] http://www.cnn.com/2013/08/09/tech/social-media/crime-social-media-psychology/

[39] http://globalnews.ca/news/1600937/luka-magnotta-surveillance-videos-released/

[40] http://globalnews.ca/news/1600025/luka-magnotta-what-did-we-learn-in-week-one-of-the-trial/

[41] http://globalnews.ca/news/1653583/german-psychiatrist-who-treated-magnotta-in-2012-testifies-for-defence/

[42] http://globalnews.ca/news/1653583/german-psychiatrist-who-treated-magnotta-in-2012-testifies-for-defence/

[43] http://globalnews.ca/news/1665435/magnotta-admitted-to-psychiatrist-he-made-up-rumour-about-karla-homolka-liaison/

[44] http://globalnews.ca/news/1676090/magnotta-trial-enters-8th-week/

[45] http://globalnews.ca/news/251318/timeline-of-events-the-luka-rocco-magnotta-case/

[46] http://globalnews.ca/tag/luka-magnotta-trial/

[47] http://www.cbc.ca/news/canada/montreal/jun-lin-was-family-s-pride-and-joy-1.1145475

[48] http://www.cbc.ca/m/touch/canada/montreal/story/1.2882819

# LUKA MAGNOTTA:
# The Cannibal Porn Star
### *Volume V*

**by Cara Lee Carter**

**Crimes Canada**
**True Crimes That Shocked The Nation**

Copyright and Published (2015)
by
VP Publications an imprint of
RJ Parker Publishing, Inc.

*Published in Canada*

Manufactured by Amazon.ca
Bolton, ON